Previously published…

- Maths and Calculator skills for Science Students
  http://amzn.to/2xgED3Q
- Maths (The Chemistry bits) for GCSE Science   May 2016
  http://amzn.to/2jJxyWc
- Science revision Guide   April 2017
  http://amzn.to/2fS0pD2
- Maths Revision Guide   April 2017
- Summer Start for A-Level Chemistry   May 2017
  http://amzn.to/2suR1e5
- Atoms, Electrons, Structure and Bonding Workbook   June 2017
  http://amzn.to/2tn8Rji
- GCSE Maths Grade 7, 8 and 9 Revision Questions   September 2017
  http://amzn.to/2fGQrrz

Coming soon…

- Complete Maths workbook
- Organic Chemistry Workbook
- Maths for A-Level Chemistry
- Maths (The Physics bits) for GCSE Combined Science
- Maths (The Physics bits) for GCSE Triple Science
- Summer Start for A-Level Physics

Chances are if you want a maths/science book I've written it or I am writing it.

For full book listings visit www.PrimroseKitten.com and follow @primrose_kitten

First published 2017   Copyright; Primrose Kitten ©

Images By Soleil Nordic used under license from Shutterstock.com. Image Courtesy NASA/JPL-Caltech.

Acknowledgements
Thank you to my husband for putting up with my spending every night writing this and for correcting all of my SPG mistakes. To my sons for being the inspiration behind Primrose Kitten.
Thank you to Ciara for getting me to write this book!

Hello Lovely Kittens

Thank you so much for purchasing this revision booklet. Many items covered in here is also included in a corresponding set of videos which I have made neat and accessible on my terrific partner platform: TuitionKit.

On TuitionKit, you'll be able to schedule many of my revision videos and partner content to help you organise your revision better, breaking it down into easy to handle bitesize chunks. You'll also find many of my other playlists and great resources from other Science and Maths teachers, as well as super English teachers too.

My videos are free when you sign up at www.tuitionkit.com/primrosekitten Using the discount code "kitten" will also give you a 20% discount on all the other material on the site for all your core GCSE subject revision.

To get a flavour for how TuitionKit's great features will help you revise, go to www.tuitionkit.com and sign up for your free 48-hour trial.

Wishing you all the best with your revision!

Primrose Kitten
xoxo

Table of Contents

Exam command words

Command words are words in exam questions that give you clues on what the examiners are looking for.

Depending on the command word, your answer to a question will vary.

There are four main ones you'll come across; give, describe, explain and evaluate.

Give what is in the picture.

For this answer, you simply need to state using one or two words what is in the picture.

<u>A dress</u>

Describe what is in the picture.

For this answer, you need to tell the examiners what it looks like or recall an event or process.

<u>An orange halter neck dress with a pale band around the waist.</u>

Explain what is in the picture.

For this answer, you need to give reasons why something is the way it is.

<u>The dress is a summer dress, so it has a halter neck, it is from the 1950s and shows the style at the time.</u>

Evaluate what is in the picture.

Here you need to give good points, bad points, your opinion and justify it.

- <u>This dress is good because it is made from a light fabric so it will be cool in the summer</u>
- <u>This dress is bad because the colour is too bright</u>
- <u>Overall, I think this is a good dress…</u>
- <u>… because it is well suited to the purpose of being a summer dress.</u>

Glossary of exam command words

Calculate/ Determine use maths to work out the answer
Choose circle the answer from the selection
Compare what are the similarities and differences
Complete fill in the gaps - pay attention to any given words, some may be used more than once some not at all
Define what does the word mean?
Describe what it looks like, or recall an event or process
Design/ Plan plan something
Draw draw a scientific diagram, not an arty sketch
Estimate give a sensible guess
Evaluate give good points, bad points your option and justify your opinion
Explain give reasons why something is the way it is
Give/Name a short answer
Identify/Label name a part
Justify give and answer and support it with a reason
Measure you might need to get your ruler out for this one
Plan write a method, don't forget your variables, controls and risk assessment
Plot mark points on a graph using an x
Predict/suggest what do you think is going to happen, you may need to use information

How to answer 6-mark questions

1. Identify the command word; this tells you what the examiners are looking for. This is generally described, explain or evaluate.
2. Go back over the question and use different colour highlighter pens to pick out key bits of information.
3. Plan the structure of your question. Table, paragraphs, diagram.
4. Write your answer
5. Check if your answer fully answers the question, and make sure it is balanced and covers all the points needed in the question.
6. Check your spelling, punctuation and grammar.

How the examiners will mark your work
- Marks are awarded on holistic judgements
- They read through the whole answer
- Judge if it is a low, middle or high-level answer
- Does your answer meet all of the requirements for the level, or only some? This will decide if the mark is towards the top of the range for the level or the bottom.

Level 1 (low-level answer) 1-2 marks
- Basic understanding of science involved
- Lacks detail
- Gaps in sequence
- Stages not in order
- Lots of irrelevant information
- Lack of connections between points

Level 2 (mid-level answer) 3-4 marks
- Understanding of scientific ideas is shown
- Only a few inaccuracies
- Nearly all detail is present
- Mostly good structure
- Mostly clear and coherent answer
- Only minor points missing

Level 3 (high-level answer) 5-6 marks
- Accurate information
- Relevant information
- Fully detailed
- Good structure
- Clear and coherent answer
- Logical answer
- Statements are clearly linked to evidence

Biology

1 - Drugs

Drugs are taken daily by a wide range of people, from legal drugs that save lives to illegal drugs that take lives, and everything in-between. There are many different types of drugs. Describe, with examples, the different types of drugs and their effects.

Planning....
- Command word; **Describe** what it looks like or recall an event or process.
- What are the 3 different types of drugs
- Gives examples of each type of drug
- Describe what each drug does.

2 - Respiration

Marathon runners and sprint runners are both exhausted after a race, but the biology behind how respiration works in these runners is very different. Compare respiration in marathon runners and sprint runners.

Planning....
- Command word; **Compare** what are the similarities and differences
- What type of respiration happens in marathon running?
- What are the reactants?
- What are the products?
- How much energy is released?
- What is the recovery?
- What type of respiration happens in Sprint running?
- What are the reactants?
- What are the products?
- How much energy is released?
- What is the recovery?

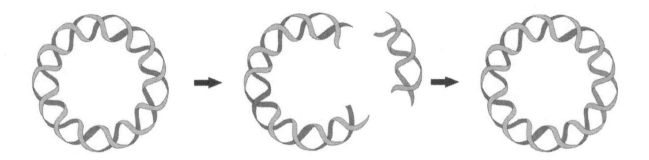

Type 1 diabetics don't produce enough insulin. In 1921, dog insulin was first purified and given to humans; this was a massive break though saving millions of lives; however, injecting dog insulin every day was not an ideal situation. It took until 1982 before human insulin became available for injection, this human insulin was not purified but made by genetically modified bacteria. Describe how human insulin can be made by genetic engineering.

Planning….

- The first part is just context, and will gain you no marks
- Command word; **Describe** what it looks like or recall an event or process.
- How does human insulin get made?
- How is genetic engineering involved?

4 – Plant Growth

The climate in the UK is very changeable, but farmers need to ensure a reliable supply of produce. To help ensure that they can provide shops with a continuous supply of food, some farmers use poly-tunnels to control the environment that food is grown in. And note that the levels of carbon dioxide, water and temperatures can be controlled inside a poly-tunnel. Explain how controlling the levels of carbon dioxide, water and the temperature will affect the growth of plants.

Planning....
- Command word; Explain give reasons why something is the way it is.
- What process give plants the required energy to grow?
- Give the equation
- How does carbon dioxide affect this?
- How does water affect this?
- How does temperature affect this?

5 – Digestive System

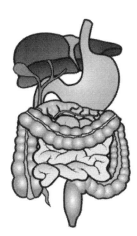

There is a range of enzymes involved in the digestive system. They have different roles and work in different places. Describe the range of enzymes that work within the digestive system.

Planning....
- Command word; **Describe** what it looks like or recall an event or process.
- There are 3 enzymes you need to name, the state where they are produced and finally where they act.

6 – Reflex Arcs

If you touch a hot object, you will withdraw your hand before you have a chance to think about it. <mark>Describe how a reflex arc works.</mark>

Planning….
- Command word; **Describe** what it looks like or recall an event or process.
- What happens initially?
- What is the path?

7 - Leaves

The leaves are a complex structure, describe the <mark>structure of a leaf</mark> including the names and <mark>functions of the different cell types</mark>.

Planning….
- Command word; **Describe** what it looks like or recall an event or process.
- What is the overall structure of the leaf like?
- What cells are within a leaf? What do they do?

8 - Pathogens

If you become infected with a pathogen, you may start to feel very ill very quickly. Compare the <mark>three different types of pathogens</mark>.

Planning….
- Command word; **Compare** what are the similarities and differences
- What are the three different types?
- How do the replicate?
- How do they make a person feel ill?

9 – Genetic Testing

Sheena's mother has an inherited dominant genetic disorder, the phenotype of this disorder only becomes evident in a person late 60's. Sheena has been offered genetic testing to see if she carries the gene for this genetic disorder. Evaluate the use of genetic testing.

Planning….

- Command word; **Evaluate** and give good points, bad points, your opinion and justify it.
- What are the positive points about genetic testing (aim for at least 2)?
- What are the negatives about genetic testing (aim for at least 2)?
- You can use a table, either just for planning or your whole answer if you write in full sentences within the table.

positive points	Negative points

- What is your opinion?
- Why do you have that opinion?
- Don't stress too much about your opinion, the examiner is never going to cross examine you on this, just make an opinion up!!

10 – Contraception

Contraception can be used to prevent unwanted pregnancies, and these can be a barrier or non-barrier methods. Compare the use of barrier or non-barrier methods of contraception.

Planning….

- Command word; **Compare** what are the similarities and differences.
- What do they have in common?
- What is different about them?

11 - IVF

IVF is a method to help a person convince a baby, the NHS funds some treatment in the UK otherwise a single round of IVF treatment in the UK can cost up to £10,000. The process can take many months and can have a long-lasting effect on mental and physical health. Describe the process of creating a baby by IVF.

Planning....
- Command word; **Describe** what it looks like or recall an event or process.
- What is the process that takes place?
- What are the steps involved?
- What drugs are involved?

12 - Defence Against Pathogens

The human body has several defences against infection by pathogens. Describe these defences.

Planning....
- Command word; **Describe** what it looks like or recall an event or process.
- How does the body prevent pathogens getting in?
- What does the body do when a pathogen does get in?

Athletes from Russia were not allowed to compete in the 2018 Winter Olympics in PyeongChang, some of them competed instead as 'Olympics athletes for Russia' under the Olympics flag. The reason behind the decision not to allow Russia to enter a team was due to widespread performance-enhancing drugs taken by the athletes. Describe why these athletes might have decided to take these drugs, include the types of drugs they might have taken.

Planning....

- Command word; **Describe** what it looks like or recall an event or process.
- Why did they take the drugs?
- What type of drugs might they have taken?
- What affect do these drugs have?

Two **genetically** identical long-tailed macaques called Zhong Zhong and Hua Hua were born in a lab in China in January 2018. These monkeys were both clones of a single adult monkey. This is the first-time an animal close to humans has been cloned. Evaluate the production of clones.

Planning....

- Command word; **Evaluate** and give good points, bad points, your opinion and justify it.
- What are the positive points about cloned animals (aim for at least 2)?
- What are the negatives about cloned animals (aim for at least 2)?
- You can use a table, either just for planning or your whole answer if you write in full sentences within the table.

positive points	Negative points

- What is your opinion?
- Why do you have that opinion?
- Don't stress too much about your opinion, the examiner is never going to cross examine you on this, just make an opinion up!!

15 – Stem Cells

A baby in the womb is connected to their mother by the umbilical cord; this umbilical cord is full of stem cells. In recent years some parent have chosen to harvest the umbilical cord immediately after birth, save and store it. This is in a case when the child needs stems cell treatment in the future. Explain the need to use stem cells in medical treatment and compare the use of donor adult stem cells and stem cells harvested from a stored umbilical cord.

Planning....

- Command words; **Explain** give reasons why something is the way it is and **compare** what are the similarities and differences
- What are stem cells?
- When might a patient need stem cell treatment?
- Where do adult stem cells come from?
- What is the advantage of stem cells harvested from stored umbilical cord?

16 - Menstrual Cycle

Starting with the first day of a woman having a period, describe what happens for the next month during the menstrual cycle.

Planning....

- Command word; **Describe** what it looks like or recall an event or process.
- What hormones are involved?
- What do these hormones do?
- Where are they produced?

IVF has been helping people have babies since the 1970's. This can be single people who want to have a baby. Same-sex couples who need some assistance. Or some of the 1 in 6 mixed-sex couples in the UK will have trouble when they try to conceive a baby. The majority of the time the cause behind this remains unknown, of the known causes 50% of the time the issues is with the male partners and the other 50% of the time the issues are with the female partner. Evaluate the use of IVF in assisting people have a baby

Planning....

- Command word; **Evaluate** give good points, bad points, your opinion and justify your opinion
- What are the positive points about IVF (aim for at least 2)?
- What are the negatives about IVF (aim for at least 2)?
- You can use a table, either just for planning or your whole answer if you write in full sentences within the table

Positive points	Negative points

- What is your opinion?
- Why do you have that opinion?
- Don't stress too much about your opinion, the examiner is never going to cross examine you on this, just make an opinion up!!

18 – Cells

Explain the structure of animal and plant cells and describe the differences.

Planning....
- Command words; **Explain** give reasons why something is the way it is and **describe** what it looks like, or recall an event or process
- What organelles are in a plant cell?
- What do the organelles in a plant cell do?
- What organelles are in an animal cell?
- What do the organelles in an animal cell do?
- What are the differences between plant and animal cells?

19 – Enzymes

Enzymes are biological catalysts; they are responsible for carrying out a large number of functions with the body. Describe how an enzyme works.

Planning....
- Command word; **describe** what it looks like, or recall an event or process.
- What is the mechanism?
- How does the mechanism work?

20 – Homeostasis

It is vitally important that a narrow set of conditions are maintained inside your body so that the reactions that are needed can take place. Maintenance of the conditions is homeostasis. Describe how homeostasis achieves this.

Planning....
- Command word; **describe** what it looks like, or recall an event or process.
- What are the 3 ways that the body maintains an environment?
- How do the mechanisms work?

Blood may seem simple, but it is responsible for a large number of functions and has many different parts to it. Describe what blood is made up from and the function of each part.

Planning....
- Command word; **describe** what it looks like, or recall an event or process.
- What are the four different parts?
- What does each part do?

22 – Genetic Disorders

Cystic fibrosis is a genetic disorder. Aimee carries the gene for cystic fibrosis when she decides she is ready to have children she can choose to undergo genetic counselling and have her partner tested to see if they also carry the gene. Use a Punnett square genetic diagram to describe the chances of two carriers having a child who suffers from cystic fibrosis.

Planning....
- Draw a Punnett square
- Annotate it fully

Enzymes are biological catalysts that have many functions in daily life. From functions within the body to making baby food and washing powder. However; enzymes are very particular about the conditions they work in. Describe the optimal conditions for an enzyme to work. You can use a diagram in your answer if you wish.

Planning....

- Command word; **describe** what it looks like, or recall an event or process.
- All marks can be gained from a fully annotated diagram
- What three things affect how an enzyme works?
- What happens when these are too low?
- What happens when these are too high?

24 – Hormonal Contraception.

'The pill' is a common form of contraception, but two different types of the pill can fall under this name. Both of these are 99.9% effective but the progesterone only pill is the only one of the two that can be given to breastfeeding women. The progesterone only pill has to be taken within a 3-hour period each day and may lead to irregular bleeding, whereas the combined oestrogen and progesterone pill can be taken within a 12-hour window and leads to reduced bleeding. The combined pill has an increased risk of blood clots. Compare the use of these two methods of contraception.

Planning….
- Command word, **Compare** what are the similarities and differences.
- What are the similarities? similarities highlighted in blue
- What are the differences? progesterone pill in yellow, combined pill in pink

25 – Plants

A plant is made up of many different organ systems and within each organ system, there is a range of different tissues. These have specialised cells which are adapted to the function that they carry out. Describe the range of specialised cells that can be found within a plant.

Planning….
- Command word; **Describe** what it looks like, or recall an event or process.
- What specialist cells are there?
- What adaptations do these cells have?
- How do they suit the cells function?

Chemistry

26 – Covalent bonding

Ammonia is a small compound that has covalent bonds. Using Ammonia as an example describe how these bonds form and what properties are associated with them. You should include a diagram in your answer.

Planning….

- Command word; **Describe** what it looks like, or recall an event or process.
- You **MUST** include a drawing
- Say what moves
- Say why it moves
- Say what properties covalent compound have
- Say why covalent compound have these properties

27 – Rates of Reaction (concentration)

Describe how concentration affects rate of reaction.

Planning....

- Command word; **Describe** what it looks like, or recall an event or process

Style; Structured paragraph

Answer – Pick one phrase from each column to make a correct sentence

When...	Concentration	Increases	**The rate of reaction...**	Increases
	Temperature	Decreases		decreases
	Surface area			

Because...	Particles have	More energy	Which allows	More frequent	**Successful collisions**
	There are less particles	Less energy	allow	less	
	There are more particles	To collide with			
		That			

28 – Atoms and Ions

How does the structure of a fluorine atom compare to the structure of a fluoride ion?

Planning....

- Command word; **Compare** what are the similarities and differences.
- What are the 3 subatomic particles?
- Where are they located?
- How many of each in a fluorine atom?
- How many of each in a fluoride ion?

29 – Magnesium Chloride

Magnesium chloride is a salt that can be made from magnesium metal and hydrochloric acid. When removed from solution it will be a white crystalline powder. Explain the properties of this compound and how it relates to the bonding of magnesium chloride. You should include the formula of the salt and a diagram.

Planning....

- The first two sentences are full of chemistry that you know a lot about, but they are not related to the final question.
- Command word; **Explain** give reasons why something is the way it is
- Give the formula of magnesium chloride
- Draw a diagram of the bonding
- State what moves
- Where does it move from?
- Where does it move to?
- How many move?
- Why do they move?

Below are 10 facts about ten unknown metals, you should use these and your knowledge of the reactivity series to put the metals in order.

1. F reacts with vigorously with water and the metal oxide forms within seconds
2. E is found in the grounds as a pure metal
3. In a very slow reaction I can displace C from a compound
4. Three of letters are in alphabetical order
5. B is reacted with C sulfate and the reaction ends in B sulfate and pure C being formed
6. J is the fourth most reactive metal
7. When H sulfate and A are reacted together the products are A sulfate and H
8. G sits 2 below J and 2 above I
9. I and C are rare precious metals that are used as jewellery, but they are both more reactive than E
10. Both B and D will displace J from a compound, but B will displace it faster

Planning….
- Cross out each fact once you have used it
- Don't expect them to be used in order

31 – Extracting Copper

There is an increasing need for copper in today's society. Subsequently, prices for copper have gone up. The increase in price has led to an increase in recycling and an increase in theft of copper from public buildings. New ways of extracting copper from low yield ores have been developed, describe and evaluate the use of bioleaching and phytomining.

Planning....

- Most of the words in this are irrelevant.
- Command word; **Describe** what it looks like, or recall an event or process and **Evaluate** give good points, bad points your option and justify your opinion
- Describe the process of bioleaching.
- Describe the process of phytomining.
- Use a table to plan out the answer

	Advantages	Disadvantages
Bioleaching	X2	X2
Phytomining	X2	X2

- Give your opinion and justify it.

Describe how temperature affects rate of reaction.

Planning....

- Command word; **Describe** what it looks like, or recall an event or process

Style; Structured paragraph

Answer – Pick one phrase from each column to make a correct sentence

When...	Concentration	Increases	The rate of reaction...	Increases
	Temperature	Decreases		decreases
	Surface area			

Because...	Particles have	More energy	Which allows	More frequent	**Successful collisions**
	There are less particles	Less energy	allow	less	
	There are more particles	To collide with			

33 - Water

Potable water is essential to a healthy life, but today 844 million people do not have access to safe, clean drinking water, and in large parts of the world, more people have access to a mobile phone than they do to a toilet. This is a problem that affects women and children disproportionally, and it is common in developing countries for women and children to spend up to 6 hours each day fetching and carrying large buckets of water on their back. Describe what portable water is and explain how contaminated water can be made into portable water.

Planning....

- Millions of people having to drink water that is contaminated with pathogens that might kill them is a very serious problem in today's world. But the first few sentences will not gain you any marks in the exam and are just to give context.
- Command words; **Describe** what it looks like or recall an event or process and **Explain** give reasons why something is the way it is.

34 – Properties of mystery white powders

Three white powders have arrived in a lab; they are labelled A, B and C. the second set of labels has fallen off. The second set of labels identify one as a simple covalent compound (wax) one as a giant covalent compound (silicon dioxide) and one as an ionic compound (salt). Design a safe experiment to distinguish between these three mystery white powders. You should include your expected results.

Planning....

- Command word; **Design-** plan something
- What are the properties of simple covalent compounds? How can we test for these?
- What are the properties of giant covalent compounds? How can we test for these?
- What are the properties of ionic compounds? How can we test for these?
- Draw a predicted results table

35 – Fractional Distillation

Estimates in the International Journal of Oil, Gas and Coal Technology suggest that we have removed almost 1 trillion barrels of crude oil from the Earth. When crude oil is removed from the ground, it is a thick sludge that can't be used for much. To turn this thick sludge into a format that can be used we need to treat the crude oil. Describe the process for fractional distillation that will turn the sludge of crude oil into useful fractions.

Planning....
- Command word; **Describe** what it looks like, or recall an event or process.
- What is crude oil made up from?
- What happens to crude oil?
- How does it become fractions?

36 – Diamond and Graphite

Explain the difference between diamond and graphite, reference their bonding, structure and properties.

Planning....
- Command word; **Explain** give reasons why something is the way it is.
- Bonding in diamond
- Structure of diamond
- Properties of diamond
- Bonding in graphite
- Structure of graphite
- Properties of graphite

$$2A_3 + B_2 \rightleftharpoons 2A_3B$$

Shown here is a reaction for a hypothetical situation, where the forward reaction is exothermic. Regarding temperature, pressure and concentration, explain the optimal conditions for the production of A_3B? Exact numbers are not expected, general terms (high/low) can be used.

Planning....

- Command word; **Explain** give reasons why something is the way it is.
- Which side do we want to reaction to go towards?
- How can we change temperature to shift the reaction this way?
- How can we change pressure to shift the reaction this way?
- How can we change concentration to shift the reaction this way?

38 – Evolution of Atmosphere

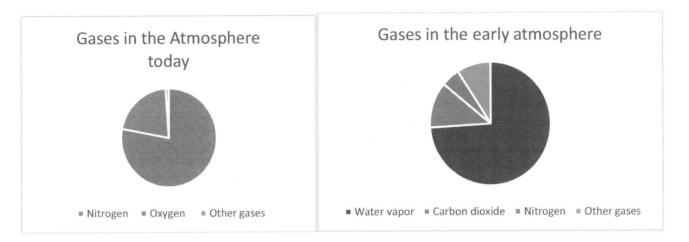

The composition of today's atmosphere is dramatically different to the early atmosphere. Explain the differences.

Planning....

- Command word; **Explain** give reasons why something is the way it is.
- What has happened to the levels of nitrogen?
- Why have the levels of nitrogen changed?
- What has happened to the levels of oxygen
- Why have the levels of oxygen changed?
- What has happened to the levels of water vapor?
- Why have the levels of water vapor changed?
- What has happened to the levels of carbon dioxide?
- Why have the levels of carbon dioxide changed?

39 – Life Cycle Assessment

In 2105 the law changed to require shops to charge 5p for each single use carrier bag that customers used. These bags were made of thin polythene and only lasted for one use. Write a life cycle assessment for the use of these bags.

Planning....
- What is the raw material for polythene?
- Where does the raw material come from?
- How sustainable is the raw material?
- What happens to that bags after use?
- What is the environmental impact of disposing of the bags?

40 - Metals

The bronze age in Britain was between 2500BCE and 700BCE, this period (and the later iron age) were both ages of rapid social and cultural development. One of the reasons behind this was the use of metals. Gold is found as a pure metal and is not useful for weapons or cooking, but bonze is useful for weapons and cooking. Explain why.

Planning....
- The first part of the question is irrelevant waffle and designed to distract you-Don't fall for the examiners trick.
- Command word; **Explain** give reasons why something is the way it is
- Structure of gold
- Properties of gold
- Link to usefulness
- Structure of bronze
- Properties of bronze
- Link to usefulness

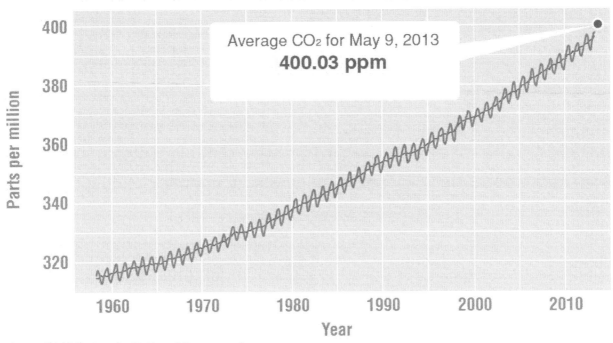

Carbon Dioxide Concentration

Average CO₂ for May 9, 2013
400.03 ppm

Parts per million

400
380
360
340
320

1960 1970 1980 1990 2000 2010

Year

Credit: NOAA/Scripps Institution of Oceanography

Image Courtesy NASA/JPL-Caltech.

The level of carbon dioxide in the atmosphere remained level for thousands of years; then in 1905, there was a sudden change. Describe and explain the pattern shown in the graph.

Planning....

- Command words; **Describe** what it looks like or recall an event or process and **Explain** give reasons why something is the way it is.
- What is the overall pattern?
- What activities are contributing to this overall pattern?
- What is the sub-pattern?
- What is causing the sub-pattern?

42 – Reactivity in Group 1 and Group 7

Sodium chloride is common table salt, lots of other salts are made of combinations of group 1 elements and group 7 elements. All of these salts look similar, they are all white crystalline solids, and the elements they are made up of have similar properties and reactions. Compare the reactions and reactivity of group 1 elements with those of group 7 elements.

Planning….

- Command word; **Compare** what are the similarities and differences.
- The first two sentence are irrelevant waffle, designed to give context but no marks.
- How do group 1 elements react?
- How do group 7 elements react?
- What is the pattern in reactivity of group 1 elements?
- What is the pattern in reactivity of group 7 elements?
- Why do group 1 elements react like they do?
- Why do group 7 elements react like they do?

43 – States of Matter

Describe the arrangement of particles in the 3 states of matter, explain how they transition between states. You may use a diagram to answer if you wish.

Planning….

- Command words; **Describe** what it looks like or recall an event or process and **Explain** give reasons why something is the way it is.
- All marks can be gained from a fully annotated diagram
- Name the 3 states
- Describe the properties of each state
- Name the transitions
- What happens to energy at each transition?

Describe how surface area affects rate of reaction.

Planning....

- Command word; **Describe** what it looks like, or recall an event or process

Answer – Pick one phrase from each column to make a correct sentence

When...	Concentration	Increases	**The rate of reaction...**	Increases
	Temperature	Decreases		decreases
	Surface area			

Because...	Particles have	More energy	Which allows	More frequent	**Successful collisions**
	There are less particles	Less energy	allow	Less	
	There are more particles	To collide with			
		That			

By 1860 a large number of elements had been discovered, so many that a way of organising them was needed. A few different ways were developed, some that made little sense and some that included non-elements. Mendeleev developed the precursor to today's periodic table, describe the advantages of his periodic table and compare it to the one we use today.

Planning….

- Command word; **Describe** what it looks like, or recall an event or process.
- How did Mendeleev organise his periodic table?
- What were the advantages of Mendeleev's periodic table over older ones?
- How is the periodic table we use today arranged?

46 – Models of the Atom

The ancient Greeks were the first to name the atom. The name they gave it (atom) means uncuttable since they thought it was the smallest thing ever. We now know that there are subatomic particles, things smaller than an atom. Describe the changes that have happened to the model of the atom over time.

Planning....

- Command word; **Describe** what it looks like, or recall an event or process.
- Describe the billiard ball model
- Describe the plum pudding model
- Describe the nuclear model
- Describe what Rutherford did
- State what Bohr added
- State what Chadwick added

47 -Group 1

Describe and explain the properties of group 1 elements

Planning....

- Command words; **Describe** what it looks like, or recall an event or process and **Explain** give reasons why something is the way it is.
- What are the properties of group 1 elements?
- What about the arrangement of the subatomic particles give rise to these properties?

Describe and explain the properties of group 7 elements

Planning….

- Command words; **Describe** what it looks like, or recall an event or process and **Explain** give reasons why something is the way it is.
- What are the properties of group 7 elements?
- What about the arrangement of the subatomic particles give rise to these properties?

49 – Aluminium Electrolysis

Explain how we get pure aluminium from its ore, you may use a diagram if you wish.

Planning….

- Command word; **Explain** give reasons why something is the way it is.
- All marks can be gained from a fully annotated diagram
- What is aluminium ore called?
- What additive is used and why?
- Where are the two electrodes placed? What are they made from?
- Give the ionic equations.
- What happens to the positive electrode?

5M Ethanoic acid is a weak acid; it is mixed with an equal volume of 0.5M sodium hydroxide which is a strong alkali. Describe a neutralisation reaction and then the difference in the solutions regarding concentration and strength.

Planning....

- Command word; **Describe** what it looks like, or recall an event or process.
- Give the neutralisation equation
- Describe the ions in a weak solution
- Describe the ions in a strong solution
- Describe the ratios in a high concentration solution
- Describe the ratios in a low concentration solution

Physics

51 – Generators

We use electricity in nearly every part of our daily life, from boiling the kettle in the morning to plugging our phones in before bed. A generator produces electricity, describe the process that happens within a generator.

Planning....

- Command word; **Describe** what it looks like, or recall an event or process.
- What is the process that happens in a generator?
- Step by step what happens.

52 – Radioactivity

Radioactivity is useful and dangerous; it needs to be carefully controlled, so it doesn't harm those using it. There are three different types of radiation, describe these different types.

Planning....

- Command word; **Describe** what it looks like, or recall an event or process.
- What are the three different types?
- What are the composed of?
- What charge do they have?
- How ionising are they?
- How much do they penetrate?

Two cars leave the same point at the same time. They travel off in different directions and encounter different traffic conditions. Compare the journeys of the two cars.

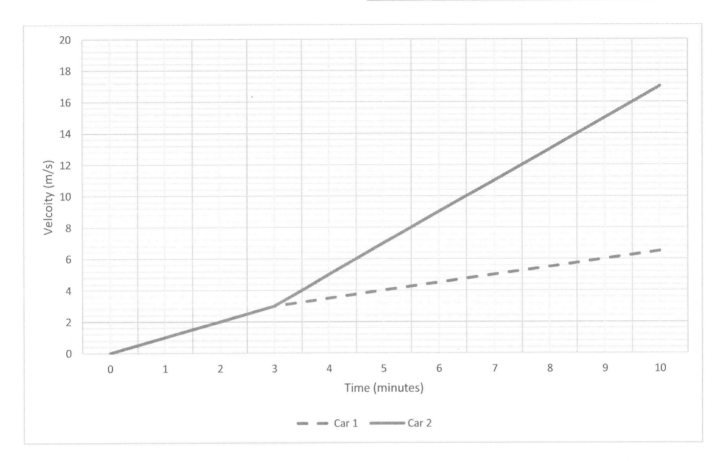

Planning....

- Command word; **Compare** what are the similarities and differences.
- What type of graph is it?
- What do the journeys have in common?
- What is different about the two journeys?
- What does the gradient of the graph tell us?
- How does the gradient change?
- Use examples from the graph
- Show working and units

54 – Thermistors

Thermistors are used in central heating systems, within a thermistor the resistance of wire changes as temperature changes. The change in resistance allows systems to turn on when it is cold and turn off at a set temperature. Explain the change in resistance of a thermistor as the temperature changes.

Planning....

- Command word; **Explain** give reasons why something is the way it is.
- How current flow through a wire?
- What is resistance?
- How does temperature affect how particles move?

55 – Nuclear Power

Nuclear power provides about 30% of Japan energy requirements. On 11th March 2011, an earthquake caused the Fukushima Daiichi Nuclear Power Plant in Ōkuma, Japan to explode. Over the next week, high levels of radioactivity leaked from the plant, over 100,000 people were evacuated from their homes to avoid exposure. While people were killed due to the earthquake, no one has died from the power plant explosion. Evaluate the generation of energy by nuclear power.

Planning....

- Command word; **Evaluate** give good points, bad points your opinion and justify your opinion
- What are the positive points about nuclear power (aim for at least 2)?
- What are the negatives about nuclear power (aim for at least 2)?
- You can use a table, either just for planning or your whole answer if you write in full sentences within the table

Positive points	Negative points

- What is your opinion?
- Why do you have that opinion?
- Don't stress too much about your opinion, the examiner is never going to cross examine you on this, just make an opinion up!!

56 – Isotopes

We can work out the age of an object that is really old by using radioactive dating. This is because plants take up carbon dioxide in photosynthesis and turn it into sugars which can be incorporated into the structure of cells. This carbon can come in two different isotopes, and it is the level of these isotopes that will tell us how old an object is. Compare the two different isotopes of carbon, carbon-12 and carbon-14.

Planning....
- Command word; **Compare** what are the similarities and differences.
- What do carbon-12 and carbon-14 have in common?
- What is different between carbon-12 and carbon-14?

57 - Forces

When a skydiver jumps out of a plane, the forces acting upon them change as they move towards the ground. Describe the different forces acting on a skydiver.

Planning....
- Command word; **Describe** what it looks like, or recall an event or process.
- What forces are acting at the beginning?
- What forces are acting on the way down?
- What forces are acting when the parachute opens?

In June 2017, for the first time, over 50% of energy in the UK was supplied by renewable energy. The UK government is leading a drive to promote the increased use of renewable energy sources for generating electricity. Evaluate the use of renewable and non-renewable energy sources.

Planning….

- **Evaluate** give good points, bad points, your opinion and justify your opinion.
- You can use a table for planning

	Good points	Bad points
Renewable energy	X2	X2
Non- renewable energy	X2	X2

- What are the good points (aim for at least 2)?
- What are the bad points (aim for at least 2)??
- What is your opinion?
- Explain why you have that opinion
- Don't stress too much about your opinion, the examiner is never going to cross examine you on this, just make one up.

59 - AC/DC

There are two types of electricity AC and DC. While Thomas Edison is widely credited with discovering electricity, he worked with DC. Nikola Tesla is actually the one we need to thank for how we got electricity in our homes today. Thomas Edison continually ridiculed Tesla and his AC system launching a campaign against him, falsely claiming it was dangerous and setting out to stop it being Developed. Nikola Tesla was brilliant but made some interesting life choices. He was in love with a pigeon and claimed to have invented a death ray. Compare the use of DC and AC current.

Planning....

- Command word; **Compare** what are the similarities and differences.
- What do they have in common?
- What is different between the two?
- Where are they used?

60 - Surfaces

Team USA's men won the gold in Curling at the 2018 Winter Olympics in PyeongChang. Curling is a sport where large highly polished stones are pushed along the ice. People running in front of the stone, brush the ice to change the direction of the stone. The brushing of the ice melts the ice. The players wear shoes that have one smooth sole, and the other shoe has a rubber sole. Explain why the players brush the ice and wear two different shoes.

Planning....

- Command word; **Explain** give reasons why something is the way it is.
- Why does melting the ice make the stone move more easily?
- Why do the shoes have different soles?
- What surfaces move over each other easily?
- Which surfaces don't move over each other easily?

61 - Car Safety

Seat belts in cars were not made compulsory in the UK until 1983, before this 6,000 people a year died in traffic accidents. Since then the number has decreased year on year until in 2015 1,732 people were killed in car accidents. Seat belts are not the only safety features in cars. Describe some the safety features that are in modern cars.

Planning….

- Command word; **Describe** what it looks like, or recall an event or process.
- Seat belts are mentioned in the question so will gain no marks.
- Give an equation, remember in physics equations are key!
- What is in the front of the car?
- What is on the dashboard?

62 – Climate Change

Fossil fuel power stations are the main source of electricity for the UK (for the time being). They are well established and serve our energy needs, but they are not without their critics. Fossil fuel power stations pump a large amount of waste gas into the atmosphere. Describe the impact these waste gases have on human life.

Planning….

- Command word; **Describe** what it looks like, or recall an event or process.
- What are the gases released? (not just carbon dioxide)
- What happens when they enter the atmosphere?
- How do they affect humans, plant and animal life?

63 - Heating

Water can be heated using either a boiler that is connected to a gas supply or by solar heating which relies on the sun. There are advantages and disadvantages to both methods, compare these methods.

Planning....

- Command word; **Compare** what are the similarities and differences.
- You can use a table, either just for planning or your whole answer if you write in full sentences on the table.

	Advantages	Disadvantages
Gas heating	X2	X2
Solar heating	X2	X2

- What are the advantages of gas heating (try to aim for at least 2)?
- What are the disadvantages of gas heating (try to aim for at least 2)?
- What are the advantages of solar heating (try to aim for at least 2)?
- What are the disadvantages of solar heating (try to aim for at least 2)?

64 – National Grid

The National grid transfers electricity from the power station to our homes. Part of this system is made up of overhead and underground power cables. Describe the advantages and disadvantages of overhead and underground power cables.

Planning....

- Command word; **Describe** what it looks like, or recall an event or process.
- You can use a table, either just for planning or your whole answer if you write in full sentences on the table.

	Advantages	Disadvantages
Overhead	X2	X2
Underground	X2	X2

- What are the advantages of overhead (try to aim for at least 2)?
- What are the disadvantages of overhead (try to aim for at least 2)?
- What are the advantages of underground (try to aim for at least 2)?
- What are the disadvantages of underground (try to aim for at least 2)?

65 - Energy Changes

Bungee jumping involves connecting an elastic cord to a person and that person jumping off a tall object. Some energy changes happen during the fall. Describe the energy changes that happen during a jump. You should include the type of energy, and a description of the different stages (before jumping, on the way down, at the bottom and on the way up).

Planning....

- Command word; **Describe** what it looks like, or recall an event or process.
- What energy is there at the start?
- What does it change on the way down?
- What energy is there at the bottom?
- How does it change on the way back up?
- Why does the bungee eventually stop?

66 - Diodes

Explain the shape of a current-potential difference graph for a diode. You should include a sketch in your answer.

Planning....

- Command word; **Explain** give reasons why something is the way it is and **Sketch** a rough drawing, a graph doesn't always need number labels on the axis, but it must be an accurate representation.
- Sketch the graph and label the axis
- Why is it that shape?
- Describe any changes in the graph

67 - Circuits

Current, resistance and potential difference behave differently in series and parallel circuits. Describe these differences.

Planning....
- Command word; **Describe** what it looks like, or recall an event or process.
- How does current behave in a series circuit?
- How does resistance behave in a series circuit?
- How does potential difference behave in a series circuit?
- How does current behave in a parallel circuit?
- How does resistance behave in a parallel circuit?
- How does potential difference behave in a parallel circuit?

68 - Waves

A Wave can be either transverse or longitudinal. While the two different types of waves have a lot in common, they also have some important differences. Describe the two different types of waves. You may use a diagram to help your answer.

Planning....
- Command word; **Describe** what it looks like, or recall an event or process.
- This can be answered using a fully annotated diagram
- What shape does each wave take?
- What are the key points that need to be labelled?
- What is the direction of movement?
- What is the direction of energy transfer?

69 – Electromagnetic Spectrum

Electromagnetic waves are all around us; they flow invisibly through the air. They have been harnessed to improve our lives in many different ways. Explain how three parts of the spectrum are used in everyday life.

Planning....

- Command word; **Explain** give reasons why something is the way it is.
- Listing part of the EM spectrum is not enough to get marks.
- To get full marks three different part must be explained, there is no point listing four.
- For each part you have chosen give how it is used in everyday life.

70 - Loudspeakers

A moving coil loudspeaker will turn electricity into sound. Explain how this works.

Planning....

- Command word; **Explain** give reasons why something is the way it is.
- What is inside a speaker?
- How do they create sound?
- How do they move?

71 - Waves

When a wave meets a solid object, the waves will bounce back. However, if there is a gap in the barrier, then the wave will pass through that gap, as it passes through the gap the properties of the wave changes. Describe how the properties of a wave will changes as it passes through a narrow gap or through a wide gap. You may use a diagram in your answer.

Planning....
- Command word; **Describe** what it looks like, or recall an event or process.
- A fully annotated diagram can be used to answer this question.
- What is the process called?
- What happens to the wave as it goes through a narrow gap?
- What happens to the wave as it goes through a wide gap?

72 – Newton's Laws of Motion

Isaac Newton lived between 1642 and 1727. He is credited with discovering gravity after an apple fell on his head and later formulating the Laws of Motion. Newton's First Law of Motion refers to balanced forces acting upon an object; while Newton's Second Law of Motion refers to unbalanced forces acting upon an object. Using examples, explain the differences between Newton's First Law of Motion and Newton's Second Law of Motion.

Planning....
- Command word; **Explain** give reasons why something is the way it is.
- How does the First law relate to stationary objects?
- How does the First law relate to moving objects?
- How does the Second law relate to stationary objects?
- How does the Second law relate to moving objects?

Describe how the atmosphere around the Earth changes as the distance from the Earth changes.

Planning....

- Command word; **Describe** what it looks like, or recall an event or process.
- Give an equation, remember in physics equations are key!
- What is the atmosphere like close to the Earth?
- What is the atmosphere like far away from the Earth?

74 – Weight and Mass

Weight and mass are often confused. Your home scales will measure your mass and not your weight; and while diets are designed to help you lose weight, they actually change the mass. Describe the difference between the two?

Planning....

- Command word; **Describe** what it looks like, or recall an event or process.
- Give an equation linking the two, remember in physics equations are key!
- What are the units involved?
- Can weight be changed?
- Can mass be changed?

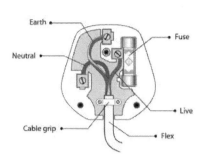

Electricity is very dangerous, shocks from faulty wiring or lightning can kill instantly. The modern house has a large number of feature to protect the user from shocks. Describe these features, including those in a plug.

Planning....

- Command word; **Describe** what it looks like, or recall an event or process.
- What can you see in the picture to talk about
- What other safety features of a plug are there?
- What other safety features around the house are there?

Answers

Q	Marking
1	First, a holistic judgement of the level of the answer must be made. The following scientific points should all be included in a level 3 answer (5-6 mark answer), just getting six points from this list does not result in a six mark answer. A drug is a chemical that changes the way the body responds Types of drugs include hallucinogens, depressants and stimulants Depressants include alcohol, relaxants and painkillers Depressants reduce the level of activity in the nervous system and the brain. Stimulants include amphetamines and cocaine Stimulants increase the level of activity in the nervous system and the brain. Hallucinogens include LSD Hallucinogens interfere with the level of activity in the nervous system and the brain leading to a distorted view of reality.
2	First, a holistic judgement of the level of the answer must be made. The following scientific points should all be included in a level 3 answer (5-6 mark answer), just getting six points from this list does not result in a six mark answer. Marathon runners use aerobic respiration Aerobic respiration can be represented by glucose + oxygen → carbon dioxide + water Aerobic respiration produces more energy per glucose Sprint runners use anaerobic respiration glucose → lactic acid can represent anaerobic respiration anaerobic respiration builds up an oxygen debt and needs heavy breathing to take in large amounts of oxygen to break down the lactic acid
3	First, a holistic judgement of the level of the answer must be made. The following scientific points should all be included in a level 3 answer (5-6

	mark answer), just getting six points from this list does not result in a six mark answer. Enzymes are used to cut out the human gene that produces insulin This is inserted into a bacterial plasmid DNA The bacteria now produce human insulin Large volumes of bacteria can be grown, producing large volumes of insulin This can be purified and used
4	First, a holistic judgement of the level of the answer must be made. The following scientific points should all be included in a level 3 answer (5-6 mark answer), just getting six points from this list does not result in a six mark answer. Plants use carbon dioxide in photosynthesis Carbon dioxide + water → oxygen + glucose Light is needed for this process carbon dioxide, water and the temperature are all limiting factors. Increasing carbon dioxide or water will increase the rate of photosynthesis but only up to a point when other factors become limiting. Temperatures are limiting if it is too low (not enough energy for the reaction to take place) or too high (enzymes denatured)
5	First, a holistic judgement of the level of the answer must be made. The following scientific points should all be included in a level 3 answer (5-6 mark answer), just getting six points from this list does not result in a six mark answer. Protease; breaks protein down into amino acids; is produced in the stomach, pancreas and small intestine; it works in the stomach and small intestine. It works best at a low pH Lipase; breaks fats into glycerol and fatty acids; made in the pancreas and small intestine; works in the small intestine. Amylase; breaks starch down into sugars; made in the salivary glands, pancreas and small intestine; works in the mouth and small intestine.

6	First, a holistic judgement of the level of the answer must be made. The following scientific points should all be included in a level 3 answer (5-6 mark answer), just getting six points from this list does not result in a six mark answer. Reflexes are very fast and are automatic; this allows the body to protect itself When touching something hot, a sensory nerve is stimulated This sensory neuron carries an impulse to the spinal cord It passes from neuron to neuron via a synapse It bypasses the brain It goes around the spinal cord via a relay neuron It travels back down a motor neuron The motor neuron will stimulate a muscle and cause a response
7	First, a holistic judgement of the level of the answer must be made. The following scientific points should all be included in a level 3 answer (5-6 mark answer), just getting six points from this list does not result in a six mark answer. Plants have a large surface area so that they can absorb lots of light The leaves are thin so that gases don't have far to diffuse They have stomata to allow gases to diffuse in and out Palisade cells are on the top surface of the leaf; these contain chlorophyll. Chlorophyll is needed for photosynthesis Spongy mesophyll cells are there to form the structure of the leaf and help to form large air spaces
8	First, a holistic judgement of the level of the answer must be made. The following scientific points should all be included in a level 3 answer (5-6 mark answer), just getting six points from this list does not result in a six mark answer. Bacteria; divide rapidly in the right conditions; release toxins that make you feel ill.

	Viruses; are the smallest of these three pathogens; replicate inside your cells, burst cells and kill them when the new viruses are released; large amounts of cell death make you feel ill. Fungi; live outside of the body; the body will react to antigens on the fungus.
9	First, a holistic judgement of the level of the answer must be made. The following scientific points should all be included in a level 3 answer (5-6 mark answer), just getting six points from this list does not result in a six mark answer. An answer cannot be level 3 if no opinion is given and back up with reasoning. Good points include; being able to plan for any future disease; certainty over what is going to happen; being able to make an informed choice about having children who may inherit the gene; Bad points include; mental health issues if testing positive, lack of healthy future; health insurance cost may increase; loss of privacy over genetic information.
10	First, a holistic judgement of the level of the answer must be made. The following scientific points should all be included in a level 3 answer (5-6 mark answer), just getting six points from this list does not result in a six mark answer. Similarities; neither is 100% effective Differences; barrier will prevent against STDs while non-barrier will not; non-barrier (hormonal) can have side effects; illness and irregular use can reduce the effectiveness of non-barrier contraception.
11	First, a holistic judgement of the level of the answer must be made. The following scientific points should all be included in a level 3 answer (5-6 mark answer), just getting six points from this list does not result in a six mark answer. Drugs are taken to prevent any eggs maturing

	High levels of FSH is injected to cause the maturation of more than one egg Eggs are removed Eggs are fertilised outside of the body (in-vitro) The fertilised egg is incubated and grown for 3-5 days The embryo/blastocyst is implanted This can then develop within the womb
12	First, a holistic judgement of the level of the answer must be made. The following scientific points should all be included in a level 3 answer (5-6 mark answer), just getting six points from this list does not result in a six mark answer. Skins act as a barrier Blood clots to stop pathogens getting in Mucous in nose and lungs traps pathogens and stops them getting into the body. White blood cells can ingest a pathogen; it recognises the pathogen, engulfs the pathogen, kills the pathogen White blood cells can produce antitoxins to counteract any toxins produced White blood cells can produce antibodies so that they can recognise pathogens faster
13	First, a holistic judgement of the level of the answer must be made. The following scientific points should all be included in a level 3 answer (5-6 mark answer), just getting six points from this list does not result in a six mark answer. Athletes may take performance-enhancing drugs to; build muscle faster; reduce anxiety before a performance; reduce pain so they can keep playing. Steroids; build muscles faster and speed up recovery time Painkillers; to be able to keep playing Stimulants; increase heart rate and speed up reaction time Anxiety reducing drugs

| 14 | First, a holistic judgement of the level of the answer must be made. The following scientific points should all be included in a level 3 answer (5-6 mark answer), just getting six points from this list does not result in a six mark answer.

An answer cannot be level 3 if no opinion is given and backed up with reasoning.

Good points; all subjects are identical, removing any difference in results due to variation; can progress research into complicated disease faster;
Bad points; clones are all genetically identical so will all be susceptible to the same diseases; expensive and time consuming to produce. |
|---|---|
| 15 | First, a holistic judgement of the level of the answer must be made. The following scientific points should all be included in a level 3 answer (5-6 mark answer), just getting six points from this list does not result in a six mark answer.

Stem cells have the potential to turn into any other type of cell
A patient might need this treatment with stems cells if they have cancer, degenerative disease or a spinal injury (other examples are acceptable)
Adult stem cells can be harvested from bone marrow, but they are in very small amounts
There are lots of stem cells in a stored umbilical cord
A patient who received donor adult stem cells may have trouble finding a matching donor and may reject the cells.
A patient who has stored umbilical cord stem cell in certain of a match and has easy access to the stem cells. |
| 16 | First, a holistic judgement of the level of the answer must be made. The following scientific points should all be included in a level 3 answer (5-6 mark answer), just getting six points from this list does not result in a six mark answer.

FSH is released from the pituitary gland |

	The FSH stimulates the release of oestrogen and the maturation of eggs Oestrogen is released from the ovaries Oestrogen causes the lining of the uterus to thicken High levels of oestrogen turn off the production of FSH and start the production of LH LH is responsible for the release of the egg from the ovary The empty follicle produces progesterone which maintains the lining of the uterus If the egg is unfertilised, the lining of the uterus will shed
17	First, a holistic judgement of the level of the answer must be made. The following scientific points should all be included in a level 3 answer (5-6 mark answer), just getting six points from this list does not result in a six mark answer. An answer cannot be level 3 if no opinion is given and backed up with reasoning. Good points; baby; parental happiness (not being able to have a baby can have a deleterious effect on mental health) Bad points; very expensive; very time consuming; large amounts of drugs have to be taken every day for months; IVF drugs lead to increased chance of cancers later in life; on 40% success rate;
18	First, a holistic judgement of the level of the answer must be made. The following scientific points should all be included in a level 3 answer (5-6 mark answer), just getting six points from this list does not result in a six mark answer. In both cells; Ribosome- make proteins Nucleus-stores DNA, control centre Cytoplasm-where reactions take place Mitochondria-produces energy Cell membrane-control what goes in and out of a cell

	In plant cells only; Vacuole-store sap Chloroplast-photosynthesis Cell wall-cell shape
19	First, a holistic judgement of the level of the answer must be made. The following scientific points should all be included in a level 3 answer (5-6 mark answer), just getting six points from this list does not result in a six mark answer. Speeds up a reaction without being used up Enzymes have an active site Only the specific substrate will fit into the active site Within the active site, the enzyme binds to the reactant The enzyme will carry out its function, either breaking the reactant into smaller parts or building it up. The products are released from the active site The enzyme can be used again Lock and key mechanism
20	First, a holistic judgement of the level of the answer must be made. The following scientific points should all be included in a level 3 answer (5-6 mark answer), just getting six points from this list does not result in a six mark answer. Homeostasis is the maintenance of a constant internal environment If the temperature is too high, the body will respond by sweating, vasodilation and hairs lying flat If the temperature is too low, the body will respond by shivering, vasoconstriction and hairs standing on end ADH is responsible for controlling how much water the kidney reuptakes If blood glucose is too low, then the pancreas make glycogen which breaks down the stores of sugar in the liver If blood glucose is too high, the pancreas produces insulin and the liver stores the glucose.

21	First, a holistic judgement of the level of the answer must be made. The following scientific points should all be included in a level 3 answer (5-6 mark answer), just getting six points from this list does not result in a six mark answer.
	Plasma; liquid part; carries dissolved substances
	Platelets; fragments of cells; form clots
	Red blood cells; biconcave discs; no nucleus; carries oxygen
	White blood cells; immune system; kills pathogens; produces antibodies' produces antitoxins
22	First, a holistic judgement of the level of the answer must be made. The following scientific points should all be included in a level 3 answer (5-6 mark answer), just getting six points from this list does not result in a six mark answer.
	R is the dominant gene, r is the recessive gene
	Mothers phenotype=carrier
	Mothers genotype=Rr
	Mothers gametes= R and r
	Fathers phenotype=carrier
	Fathers genotype=Rr
	Father gametes= R and r

		Mothers gametes	
		R	r
Father gametes	R	RR Normal	Rr carrier
	r	Rr carrier	rr sufferer

23	First, a holistic judgement of the level of the answer must be made. The following scientific points should all be included in a level 3 answer (5-6 mark answer), just getting six points from this list does not result in a six mark answer.
	When the temperature is too low, there will be no enzyme activity, as there won't be enough energy

	When the temperature is too high, the enzymes will be denatured, so there will be no activity Optimal temperature is in-between too high and too low When pH is too high or too low the enzyme will be denatured so will not work When substrate concentration is too low, this will limit the amount of activity When substrate concentration is high than enzyme concentration, it won't have any effect as the enzyme is limiting
24	First, a holistic judgement of the level of the answer must be made. The following scientific points should all be included in a level 3 answer (5-6 mark answer), just getting six points from this list does not result in a six mark answer. Similarities; both 99.9% effective; both need to be taken every day Differences; progesterone only needs to be taken within a 3-hour window, combined within a 12-hour window; progesterone only is the only one that can be taken by breastfeeding women; combined pill can lead to blood clots; progesterone only can lead to irregular bleeding
25	First, a holistic judgement of the level of the answer must be made. The following scientific points should all be included in a level 3 answer (5-6 mark answer), just getting six points from this list does not result in a six mark answer. Root hair cells; have thin walls and a large surface area to allow water to pass into the roots easily; form a large network to help keep the plant in the solid. Leaves; have a large surface area to absorb lots of light, have palisade cells with large amounts of chlorophyll for photosynthesis; stomata and guard cells allow gases to diffuse in and out; spongy mesophyll has a large structure to create air spaces. Stem; phloem cells transport sugars around the plant; xylem cells are hollow to allow water and minerals to move up (up only) from the root.

| 26 | First, a holistic judgement of the level of the answer must be made. The following scientific points should all be included in a level 3 answer (5-6 mark answer), just getting six points from this list does not result in a six mark answer. |
| | |

Covalent bonding is the sharing of electrons
So that each element has a full outer shell
Covalent compounds have strong intramolecular bonds
Covalent compounds have weak intermolecular bonds
Weak intermolecular bonds do not require much energy to overcome these bonds
The weak intermolecular bonds mean that covalent compounds have low boiling points and low melting points.

| 27 | When concentration increases, the rate of reaction increases because there are more particles to collide with which allow more frequent successful collisions

OR

When concentration decreases, the rate of reaction decreases because there are fewer particles to collide with which allow less frequent successful collisions |

| 28 | First, a holistic judgement of the level of the answer must be made. The following scientific points should all be included in a level 3 answer (5-6 mark answer), just getting six points from this list does not result in a six mark answer.

An ion is an atom that has lost or gained electrons
Protons are in the nucleus |

Neutrons are in the nucleus

Electrons are on the outer shells

A fluorine atom has 9 protons, 10 neutrons and 9 electrons

A fluoride ion has 9 protons, 10 neutrons and 10 electrons

| 29 | First, a holistic judgement of the level of the answer must be made. The following scientific points should all be included in a level 3 answer (5-6 mark answer), just getting six points from this list does not result in a six mark answer. |

MgCl$_2$. Do not accept any other answer, do not accept wrong sized numbers or incorrect capitalisation of letters

A magnesium atom has two electrons in its outer shell

It needs to lose two electrons to have a full outer shell

Ions with a full outer shell are more stable

Its loses these electrons to form a 2+ ion

A chlorine atom has 7 electrons in it outer shell

It needs one more electron to complete its outer shell

A chloride ion forms

Chloride has a 1- charge

Two chlorine atoms bond with one magnesium atom

Between the negative and the positive ions, an electrostatic attraction has formed

| 30 | F, B, D, J, A, G, H, I, C, E |

| 31 | First, a holistic judgement of the level of the answer must be made. The following scientific points should all be included in a level 3 answer (5-6 mark answer), just getting six points from this list does not result in a six mark answer.

To get above 4 marks an opinion with linked reason must be given.

Phytomining is using plants to draw copper out of the soil, via their roots, burning the plants and extracting the copper (via electrolysis) from the ash
Advantages are; getting copper from the soil, low set up the cost
Disadvantages are; can only grow one or two crops each year, high energy use at the end, burning plants adds carbon dioxide to the atmosphere, food could be used to feed people.
Bioleaching is using bacteria to suck up copper from large bodies of water (a lake) and extracting copper from the bacterial leachate.
Advantages are; getting copper from water, cheap to set up
Disadvantages are; slow process, still needs electrolysis at the end |
|---|---|
| 32 | When the temperature increases, the rate of reaction increases because the particles have more energy which allows more frequent successful collisions

OR

When the temperature decreases, the rate of reaction decreases because the particles have less energy which allows less frequent successful collisions |
| 33 | First, a holistic judgement of the level of the answer must be made. The following scientific points should all be included in a level 3 answer (5-6 mark answer), just getting six points from this list does not result in a six mark answer.

Suitable stores for drinking water, a reservoir or well, not a river
Water should be filtered to remove large debris |

	Water can then be passed through smaller and smaller filters to remove particulates of mud and then bacteria A sedimentation tank can be sued to collect together a small bit of mud Chlorine can be added to kill any bacteria, or it can be heat sterilised
34	First, a holistic judgement of the level of the answer must be made. The following scientific points should all be included in a level 3 answer (5-6 mark answer), just getting six points from this list does not result in a six mark answer. The method shown actually works, e.g. they cannot test for solubility if they don't mention anywhere adding the compound to water. Do not assume steps. Test melting point Test solubility Test conduction of electricity with a bulb in a circuit

	Expected Results		
Compound	Test 1 Melting point	Test 2 Solubility	Test 3 Electricity conduction
Simple covalent	Low (melts)	Not soluble	Does not conduct
Giant covalent	High (does not melt)	Not soluble	Does not conduct
Ionic	High (does not melt)	Soluble	Conducts

35	First, a holistic judgement of the level of the answer must be made. The following scientific points should all be included in a level 3 answer (5-6 mark answer), just getting six points from this list does not result in a six mark answer. Crude oil is a mixture of different length hydrocarbons Crude oil is heated so that most of it evaporates

	The fractional distillation column is at different temperatures, cool at the top and hot at the bottom The evaporated crude oil will condense at different temperatures. Condensing points depend on the length of the hydrocarbons chain Long chains condense at the bottom Short chains condense at the top The longest chains never evaporate and will remain a liquid The shortest chains are a gas
36	First, a holistic judgement of the level of the answer must be made. The following scientific points should all be included in a level 3 answer (5-6 mark answer), just getting six points from this list does not result in a six mark answer. Diamond and graphite are both made up of pure carbon They are both giant covalent structures In diamond, each carbon makes 4 bonds The bonds in diamond are very strong Strong bonds require large amounts of energy to break, giving the diamond a high melting and boiling point Diamond is very hard due to its large structure In graphite, each carbon marks 3 carbon-carbon bonds The carbons atoms are arranged in layers These layers can slide over each other Thus, graphite is soft The 4th electron is delocalised between the layers of graphite The delocalised electron means graphite can conduct electricity.
37	First, a holistic judgement of the level of the answer must be made. The following scientific points should all be included in a level 3 answer (5-6 mark answer), just getting six points from this list does not result in a six mark answer. The forward reaction is exothermically suggesting a low temperature needed to shift the reaction to the right-hand side. There are more moles on the left-hand side so that a high pressure would shift the reaction to the right-hand side.

	Increasing the concentration of the reactants would shift the reaction to the right-hand side.
38	First, a holistic judgement of the level of the answer must be made. The following scientific points should all be included in a level 3 answer (5-6 mark answer), just getting six points from this list does not result in a six mark answer. The early atmosphere developed due to volcanic eruptions The levels of nitrogen in the atmosphere have increased, this is due to ammonia reacting with oxygen and nitrogen gas being released. The levels of water vapour have decreased as it rained and created the oceans The levels of carbon dioxide have decreased as the carbon dioxide dissolved in the oceans, was locked up in rocks and fossils and was taken up by plants during photosynthesis. The levels of oxygen have increased due to photosynthesis.
39	First, a holistic judgement of the level of the answer must be made. The following scientific points should all be included in a level 3 answer (5-6 mark answer), just getting six points from this list does not result in a six mark answer. Polythene is a polymer of ethene, Ethene is a hydrocarbon chain The raw material of polythene bags is crude oil. Crude oil is a finite resource and is not sustainable After use, the bags will go to the landfill where they will last for thousands of years. Bags can be incinerated, this releases large amounts of carbon dioxide into the atmosphere but can provide energy which can be useful. Animals can eat the bags causing death or health problems.
40	First, a holistic judgement of the level of the answer must be made. The following scientific points should all be included in a level 3 answer (5-6 mark answer), just getting six points from this list does not result in a six mark answer.

	Pure metals are made of one type of element
	All particles in a pure metal are the same size
	In a pure metal, the particles are arranged in layers
	In a pure metal, the layers can slide across each other
	When layers slide across each other, the metal is soft
	Pure metals are not good for weapons or cooking as they are too soft
	Bronze is not a pure metal; it is not on the periodic table
	Bronze is an alloy
	In an alloy, there is a mixture of different elements
	The particles in an alloy are all different sizes
	The different sized particles in an alloy mean the layers are distorted
	Distorted layers cannot slide
	The distorted layers mean an alloy is hard
	Alloys are good as weapons as they are hard
41	First, a holistic judgement of the level of the answer must be made. The following scientific points should all be included in a level 3 answer (5-6 mark answer), just getting six points from this list does not result in a six mark answer. CO_2 can be used, but only gets credit if written correctly. Incorrect or ambiguous capitalisation or position of numbers does not get credit. Levels of carbon dioxide are increasing Human activities are causing the change in carbon dioxide levels Use of petrol and diesel in cars Burning fossils fuels for electricity Deforestation The up and down subpattern is due to the change in season. Plants lose leaves in the winter so cannot carry out photosynthesis. Photosynthesis removes carbon dioxide from the atmosphere. NB; the change in season refers to the northern hemisphere only. When it is winter in the northern hemisphere, it is summer in the southern hemisphere, but the majority of landmass (and thus plants) is in the northern hemisphere.

42	First, a holistic judgement of the level of the answer must be made. The following scientific points should all be included in a level 3 answer (5-6 mark answer), just getting six points from this list does not result in a six mark answer. Group 7 React violently Reactivity decreases as you go down the group Large elements have more electron shells The more shells, the less attraction between the nucleus and the outer electrons The harder it is to gain electrons Group 1 Violent reaction Reactivity increases as you go down the group Large elements have more electron shells The more shells, the less attraction between the nucleus and the outer electrons The larger element loses electrons more easily Melting points and boiling points decrease as you go down the group
43	First, a holistic judgement of the level of the answer must be made. The following scientific points should all be included in a level 3 answer (5-6 mark answer), just getting six points from this list does not result in a six mark answer. All marks can be gained from a fully annotated diagram Solid particles, vibrate very little around a fixed position There is only no vibrate in a solid at absolute zero Liquid particles move randomly within a proximity to each other Gas particles are widely spaced apart with rapid random movements Solid to gas is sublimation

	Solid to liquid is melting this requires energy
	Liquid to gas is evaporating this requires energy
	Gas to liquid is condensing this releases energy
	Liquid to solid is freezing this releases energy
44	When surface area increases, the rate of reaction increases because there are more particles to collide with which allows more frequent successful collisions OR When surface area decreases, the rate of reaction decreases because there are fewer particles to collide with which allows less frequent successful collisions
45	First, a holistic judgement of the level of the answer must be made. The following scientific points should all be included in a level 3 answer (5-6 mark answer), just getting six points from this list does not result in a six mark answer. Mendeleev organised his table by mass Mendeleev left gaps for yet to be discovered elements and predicted their properties. Mendeleev arranged elements into groups with similar properties Previous periodic tables mixed metals and non-metals and had no gaps Electron arrangement orders Today's periodic table
46	First, a holistic judgement of the level of the answer must be made. The following scientific points should all be included in a level 3 answer (5-6 mark answer), just getting six points from this list does not result in a six mark answer. Billiard ball – atom as a solid sphere

Plum pudding – atom as a solid sphere of positive charge with negative electrons dotted throughout

Nuclear model – atom has a central positive nucleus, with electrons around the outside

Rutherford's gold foil experiment proved the existence of a positive central nucleus

Bohr developed the nuclear model

Chadwick discovered neutrons

47	First, a holistic judgement of the level of the answer must be made. The following scientific points should all be included in a level 3 answer (5-6 mark answer), just getting six points from this list does not result in a six mark answer.

Form +1 ions

1 electron in the outer shell

Reactivity increases as you go down the group

Large elements have more electron shells

The more shells, the less attraction between the nucleus and the outer electrons

The larger element loses electrons more easily

Melting points and boiling points decrease as you go down the group

48	First, a holistic judgement of the level of the answer must be made. The following scientific points should all be included in a level 3 answer (5-6 mark answer), just getting six points from this list does not result in a six mark answer.

Diatomic molecules (F_2, Cl_2)

Form -1 ions

7 electrons in the outer shell

Melting points and boiling points increase as you go down the group

Reactivity decreases as you go down the group

Large elements have more electron shells

The more shells, the less attraction between the nucleus and the outer electrons

The harder it is to gain electrons

49	First, a holistic judgement of the level of the answer must be made. The following scientific points should all be included in a level 3 answer (5-6 mark answer), just getting six points from this list does not result in a six mark answer.

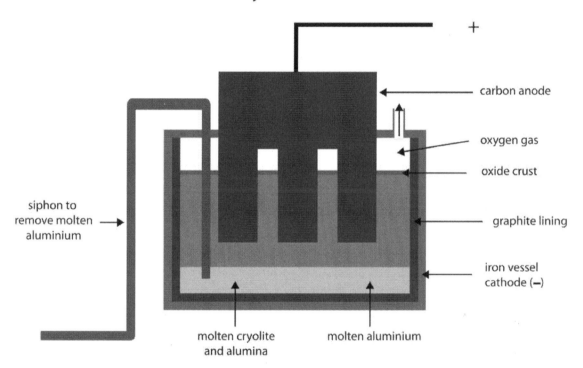

Electrolysis of Aluminium

carbon anode

oxygen gas

oxide crust

siphon to remove molten aluminium

graphite lining

iron vessel cathode (−)

molten cryolite and alumina

molten aluminium

Electrode Reactions:

At Cathode: $4Al^{3+} + 12e^- \longrightarrow 4Al$

At Anode: $6O^{2-} \longrightarrow 3O_2 + 12e^-$

Overall: $4Al^{3+} + 6O^{2-} \qquad 4Al + 3O_2$

50	First, a holistic judgement of the level of the answer must be made. The following scientific points should all be included in a level 3 answer (5-6 mark answer), just getting six points from this list does not result in a six mark answer. $H^+ + OH^- \rightarrow H_2O$

	Ions in a weak solution are partially dissociated Ions in a strong solution are fully dissociated A high concentration has lots of acid molecules for each water molecule A low concentration solution has few alkali molecules for each water molecule
51	First, a holistic judgement of the level of the answer must be made. The following scientific points should all be included in a level 3 answer (5-6 mark answer), just getting six points from this list does not result in a six mark answer. A generator is made up of a spinning coil of wire inside a magnetic field or a spinning magnet within a coil of wire An electric current is produced when a wire is passed through a magnetic field To increase the current the number of coils can be increased, or the strength of the magnet can be increased. To increase the rate that current is generated, the rate of spinning can be increased.
52	First, a holistic judgement of the level of the answer must be made. The following scientific points should all be included in a level 3 answer (5-6 mark answer), just getting six points from this list does not result in a six mark answer. Alpha radiation; has a positive charge; is a helium nucleus; made up of 2 protons and 2 neutrons; very ionising; stopped by paper, doesn't penetrate much. Beta radiation; has a negative charge; is an electron; mid-level ionisation and penetration; stopped by thin aluminium Gamma radiation; is a wave, no charge, no mass; can penetrate deeply, stopped by thick lead or concrete.
53	First, a holistic judgement of the level of the answer must be made. The following scientific points should all be included in a level 3 answer (5-6 mark answer), just getting six points from this list does not result in a six mark answer.

	Gradient of velocity time graph shows acceleration Car 1 initial acceleration is 1m/s^2, then slows to 0.5m/s^2 Car 2 initial acceleration is 1m/s^2, then speed up to 2 m/s^2 Both cars have the same initial acceleration The acceleration changes at 3 minutes
54	First, a holistic judgement of the level of the answer must be made. The following scientific points should all be included in a level 3 answer (5-6 mark answer), just getting six points from this list does not result in a six mark answer. Current is the movement of electrons through a wire Resistance is anything that slows down the movement of the current At low temperatures, there is a very little movement of particles within the wire. The lack of movement means the electrons (current) can flow freely; there is very low resistance. At high temperatures, there is lots of movement of particles within a wire. The rapid movement means the flow of electrons (current) is impaired, meaning there is high resistance.
55	First, a holistic judgement of the level of the answer must be made. The following scientific points should all be included in a level 3 answer (5-6 mark answer), just getting six points from this list does not result in a six mark answer. An answer cannot be level 3 if no opinion is given and backed up with reasoning. Good points; no carbon dioxide released; lots of energy produced; Bad points; risk of explosion; expensive to set up; non-renewable; waste needs storing for a long time;
56	First, a holistic judgement of the level of the answer must be made. The following scientific points should all be included in a level 3 answer (5-6 mark answer), just getting six points from this list does not result in a six mark answer.

	Similarities; both have 6 electrons in outer shells; both have 6 protons in the nucleus Differences; carbon-14 has 8 neutrons in the nucleus and carbon-12 has 6 neutrons in the nucleus; carbon-14 is unstable and thus radioactive, carbon-12 is stable and not radioactive.
57	First, a holistic judgement of the level of the answer must be made. The following scientific points should all be included in a level 3 answer (5-6 mark answer), just getting six points from this list does not result in a six mark answer. Just after the skydiver leaves the plane, the force of gravity pulls them downwards and causing them to accelerate. As they accelerate downwards, the upwards force of air resistance increases. Acceleration continues until the upwards force from the air resistance and the downwards force are equal When the forces are equal, and there is no more acceleration, this is the terminal velocity. Once the parachute opens the surface area increases The increase in the surface area leads to an increase in air resistance This causes the air resistance to be greater than the acceleration, and the skydiver will slow down. As the skydiver slows down the force from the air resistance reduces A new slower terminal velocity is reached as the upwards, and downwards force become balanced again.
58	First, a holistic judgement of the level of the answer must be made. The following scientific points should all be included in a level 3 answer (5-6 mark answer), just getting six points from this list does not result in a six mark answer. An answer cannot be level 3 if no opinion is given and backed up with reasoning. The answer must be a balance between the four bullet points. Renewable, good points; not going to run out; not polluting

	Renewable, bad points; building new power plants is expensive and time-consuming; not reliable. Non-renewable, good points; already established; quick startup times. Non-renewable bad points; releases carbon dioxide into the atmosphere which contributes to climate change; going to run out; other named pollution.
59	First, a holistic judgement of the level of the answer must be made. The following scientific points should all be included in a level 3 answer (5-6 mark answer), just getting six points from this list does not result in a six mark answer. AC is constantly changing direction DC flows in one direction AC is mains electricity DC is in batteries Motors work with AC Circuits work with DC AC can be stepped up and down using transformers AC can travel long distances without loss of energy DC can't be sent over long distances as they lose energy quickly AC cannot be used in portable devices
60	First, a holistic judgement of the level of the answer must be made. The following scientific points should all be included in a level 3 answer (5-6 mark answer), just getting six points from this list does not result in a six mark answer. Brushing the ice causes friction Friction causes heat Heat melts the ice, and the stone can move more easily over water as there is less friction Smooth soled shoes allow the player to slide along the ice with little friction Rubber soled shoes provide friction allowing the player to walk and not slip on the ice

61	First, a holistic judgement of the level of the answer must be made. The following scientific points should all be included in a level 3 answer (5-6 mark answer), just getting six points from this list does not result in a six mark answer. F=ma, reduction in acceleration will reduce the force on the people in the car. Airbags provide a cushion for the person moving forward reducing acceleration Crumple zones at the front of cars absorb the energy impact slowing the car down
62	First, a holistic judgement of the level of the answer must be made. The following scientific points should all be included in a level 3 answer (5-6 mark answer), just getting six points from this list does not result in a six mark answer. Carbon particles (soot); global dimming, breathing difficulties Carbon dioxide; greenhouse gas, stop infrared radiation escaping the atmosphere leading to climate change. Sulfur dioxide; mixes with clouds to produce acid rain, leads to damage to plants, buildings and aquatic life Water is a greenhouse gas
63	First, a holistic judgement of the level of the answer must be made. The following scientific points should all be included in a level 3 answer (5-6 mark answer), just getting six points from this list does not result in a six mark answer. Solar is renewable Gas is finite Solar does not contribute to climate change Burning gas releases carbon dioxide which is a greenhouse gas Gas is expensive Sun in free Gas is available all the time Sun only works on sunny days

	Gas is reliable and consistent Sun is variable
64	First, a holistic judgement of the level of the answer must be made. The following scientific points should all be included in a level 3 answer (5-6 mark answer), just getting six points from this list does not result in a six mark answer. Overhead advantages; thinner cables can be used, easy to get to if repair is needed, less expensive to install, air is an electrical insulator, cooled by air. Overhead disadvantages; Can cause a hazard to birds or flying vehicles, can be damaged by bad weather, the risk to the public of electric shock, visual pollution. Underground advantages; not in a location that can harm people or animals; little risk of electric shock; hidden from sight; not damaged by weather. Underground disadvantages; thick cables needed to protect them; installation and maintenance is expensive and involves digging up the landscape.
65	First, a holistic judgement of the level of the answer must be made. The following scientific points should all be included in a level 3 answer (5-6 mark answer), just getting six points from this list does not result in a six mark answer. Before jumping all the energy is stored as gravitational potential energy As the jump starts, energy is transferred from the store of gravitational potential energy to kinetic energy as the person stars to accelerate downwards. At the bottom of the jump, when the bungee cord is pulled tight, the kinetic energy has been transferred to a store of elastic potential energy in the cord. On the way back up the store of elastic potential energy is transferred back to kinetic energy The bungee will eventually stop as energy is lost heat as the cord extended and shortened during the jump

66	First, a holistic judgement of the level of the answer must be made. The following scientific points should all be included in a level 3 answer (5-6 mark answer), just getting six points from this list does not result in a six mark answer. 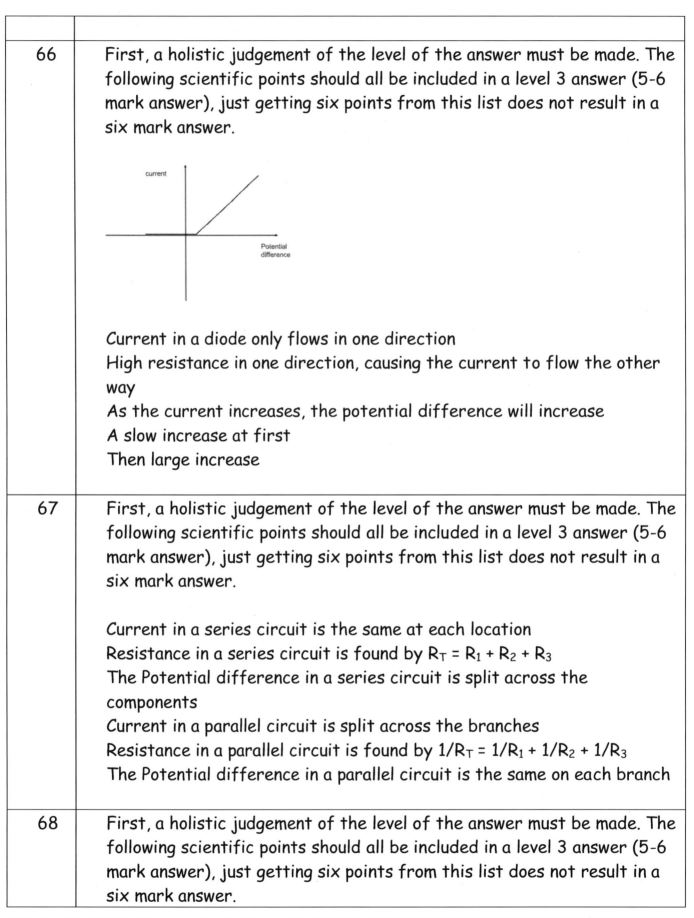 Current in a diode only flows in one direction High resistance in one direction, causing the current to flow the other way As the current increases, the potential difference will increase A slow increase at first Then large increase
67	First, a holistic judgement of the level of the answer must be made. The following scientific points should all be included in a level 3 answer (5-6 mark answer), just getting six points from this list does not result in a six mark answer. Current in a series circuit is the same at each location Resistance in a series circuit is found by $R_T = R_1 + R_2 + R_3$ The Potential difference in a series circuit is split across the components Current in a parallel circuit is split across the branches Resistance in a parallel circuit is found by $1/R_T = 1/R_1 + 1/R_2 + 1/R_3$ The Potential difference in a parallel circuit is the same on each branch
68	First, a holistic judgement of the level of the answer must be made. The following scientific points should all be included in a level 3 answer (5-6 mark answer), just getting six points from this list does not result in a six mark answer.

Waveforms

Transverse Wave

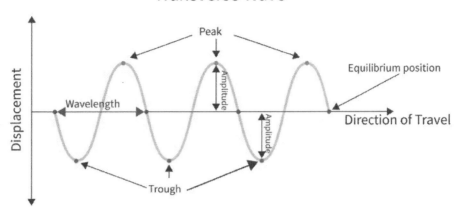

Longitudinal Wave

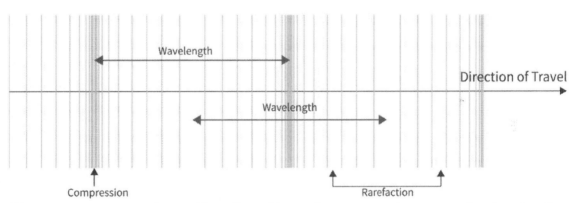

Transverse waves have the direction of movement perpendicular to the direction of energy transfer

Longitudinal waves have the direction of movement in the same direction as the direction of energy transfer.

| 69 | First, a holistic judgement of the level of the answer must be made. The following scientific points should all be included in a level 3 answer (5-6 mark answer), just getting six points from this list does not result in a six mark answer. |

	Named section of the spectrum and linked reason will gain two marks, up to a total of 6. No marks are awarded just for naming a part of the spectrum.
	Radio waves; use in communication, radios Microwaves; used in cooking, mobile phones Infrared; used for heat sensing; communication between electronic devices Visible light; used in cameras Ultraviolet; used for checking for forgeries; invisible ink X-rays; used in medicine Gamma rays; used for medical treatment; radioactive.
70	First, a holistic judgement of the level of the answer must be made. The following scientific points should all be included in a level 3 answer (5-6 mark answer), just getting six points from this list does not result in a six mark answer. Sound travels by longitudinal wave Speakers need to vibrate to create movement Speakers have both a permanent magnet and an electromagnet The pole on a permanent magnet does not change The pole of the electromagnet can be changed Switching the direction of the current switches the pole on an electromagnet This causes the permanent magnetic and the electromagnet to change between attraction and repulsion Thus, moving the speaker cone and creating a longitudinal wave
71	First, a holistic judgement of the level of the answer must be made. The following scientific points should all be included in a level 3 answer (5-6 mark answer), just getting six points from this list does not result in a six mark answer. Diffraction Large gap

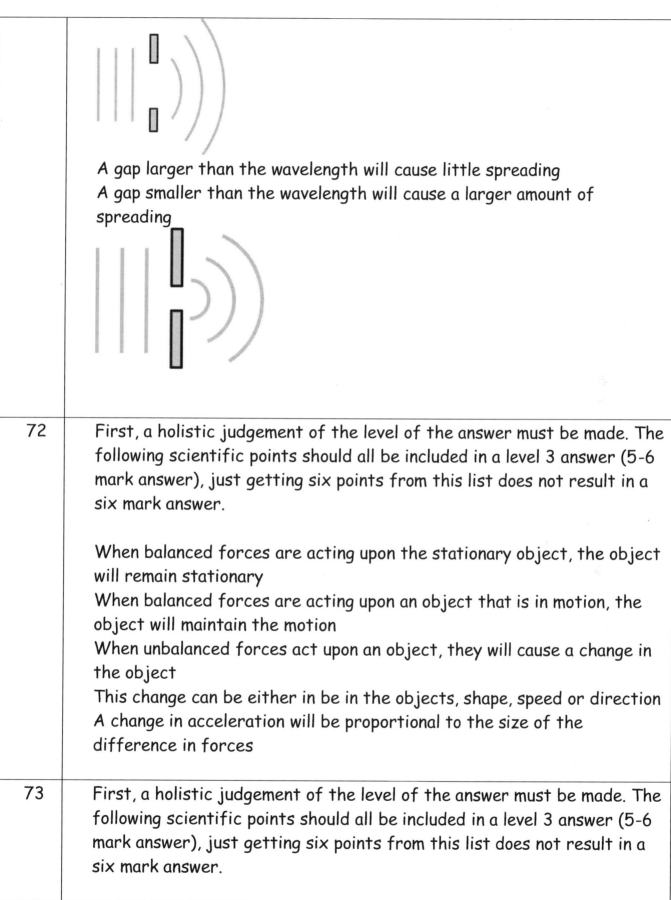

A gap larger than the wavelength will cause little spreading
A gap smaller than the wavelength will cause a larger amount of spreading

72	First, a holistic judgement of the level of the answer must be made. The following scientific points should all be included in a level 3 answer (5-6 mark answer), just getting six points from this list does not result in a six mark answer. When balanced forces are acting upon the stationary object, the object will remain stationary When balanced forces are acting upon an object that is in motion, the object will maintain the motion When unbalanced forces act upon an object, they will cause a change in the object This change can be either in be in the objects, shape, speed or direction A change in acceleration will be proportional to the size of the difference in forces
73	First, a holistic judgement of the level of the answer must be made. The following scientific points should all be included in a level 3 answer (5-6 mark answer), just getting six points from this list does not result in a six mark answer.

	The atmosphere is made of gases The atmosphere has different layers We mainly use the layer that is closest (less than 7km) $p = h\rho g$ The further you are away from the Earth, the lower the pressure.
74	First, a holistic judgement of the level of the answer must be made. The following scientific points should all be included in a level 3 answer (5-6 mark answer), just getting six points from this list does not result in a six mark answer. $W=mg$ Weight is measured in N Mass is measured in kg Weight is a vector quantity Mass is a scalar quantitated Weight will change with the force of gravity, e.g. you weigh less on the moon because gravity is less Mass doesn't change
75	First, a holistic judgement of the level of the answer must be made. The following scientific points should all be included in a level 3 answer (5-6 mark answer), just getting six points from this list does not result in a six mark answer. A plug has a fuse, which will stop electricity (current) if too much electricity flows (by getting too hot and breaking) Houses have residual current circuit breakers (RCCB) which detect surges in electricity very quick and will turn off the electricity Earth wires take current to the ground The plastic coating on outside of wires are made to insulate any form of shock Wires are double insulated

Printed in Great Britain
by Amazon

56695768R00050